Winner or Loser?

Winning Over Basic Youth Conflicts

By

Mark W. Metzger
New Teen Author

CIS Publishing Company
ARGYLE, TX 76226
WWW.CISPUBLISHING.COM

 First Edition 6/2012

The information in this book is written for educational purposes only and is not recommended as a means of diagnosing or treating any disorders mentioned within. All matters concerning social behavior, emotional stress or conditions, suicidal tendencies, mental health should be supervised by a health practitioner knowledgeable in treating that particular condition. Neither the publisher nor author directly or indirectly dispense phycological advice, nor do they prescribe any remedies or assume any responsibility for those who choose to apply the principles described in this book.

The compilation of information in this book is reprinted by permission of the author. The stories represented within this book are not fictional and represent actual incidents that occurred as recalled by the author, however,the names of the people mentioned have been changed to respect the privacy of the individuals involved.

Table of Contents:

Dedication / Author's Preface

Mark W. Metzger

The purpose of this book is to demonstrate and help people recognize the impact of their actions and words on others. It is important to appreciate and value differences. I used many stories and examples that have had a huge impact on me as an individual. Some of the stories that I used are not about "me." These stories were recounted because they fit the theme of each chapter. My hope is that as you read my book, you will find a chapter or two that will either help you with a specific problem you are facing, a need you have or impact you in some way. I hope after you read this book, that you will have a better understanding and that it is better to "build people up," instead of "knocking people down." My purpose for writing this book was to help you leave a positive impact on everyone you can!

A brief word about the names used in my stories. Out of respect for the privacy of others, I have not used the actual names of the people in their stories. My family members, on the other hand, have allowed the use of their real names.

I dedicate this book to my parents Gary and Nancy Metzger for being my absolute, best teachers. They are always lifting me up and supporting me in everything that I do. I am blessed to have such wonderful parents.

Forward

Glenn M. Bianchi, Family Friend and Mentor

When I first met Mark, he introduced himself, looking straight into my eyes, gave me a warm smile and a firm handshake. I knew he was mature far beyond his youth. This polite and confident young man knew who he was. Aside from being a true gentleman, he was also a strong athlete, who could out-skate and out-play any of the more experienced hockey players with whom he faced off.

Over the next couple of years I watched Mark grow in maturity and wisdom, a young man led by the Holy Spirit and strong in his convictions of what he believed in. He has eyes to see the needs of others and a very generous heart, giving of his time and resources to the less fortunate. He is a young man of integrity and character.

Mark has the heart of a true leader...not swayed by the world or opinions around him. Truly gifted by The Holy Spirit and respect for others, Mark has the ability in his words and actions to love and lift others up. God's Word tells us that we are not to be conformed to this world and held back by its trappings. Mark exemplifies Christ's Love in his motives and actions.

To my dear friend, Mark....Be strong and courageous in the Word of the Lord!

Publisher's Preface

Terry E. Minke - Publisher - CIS Publishing Company

When I first received the manuscript from this insightful young man, Mark Metzger, who was only 18 at the time, I was skeptical as to what life lessons he had the time to experience and the inspiration to write about. However, I soon learned and was quite amazed at the resolve he had to help others achieve a more purposeful life by sharing stories of his youth and giving other youth (and many adults as well) insightful and positive actions they could take to accomplish their goals.

As a self-publishing expert, my goal was to help Mark publish his book and to attract the right audience so that he would have the greatest impact on the largest number of people. I quickly realized that Mark had written a "Guidebook for Dealing with and Resolving Basic Youth Conflicts" to help young people become "Winners" at the game of life and not "Losers," a popular label used by youth to demean their peers.

As Life Group Leaders at our church in Argyle, Texas, my wife Donna and I have often searched the scriptures looking for inspirational stories to share with our small group or challenging subjects for future group Bible studies. After Donna had read a few sample chapters of Mark's manuscript, she remarked, "Mark should read Isaiah 53 and see how well this chapter's subject "the suffering servant's life" parallels the life of Jesus with the lives of so many young people from the past and present day." As she read Isaiah 53 to me, I understood exactly what she meant. In this Old Testament scripture, the prophet Isaiah describes a "servant" yet to come, Jesus Christ. It describes how he had no special features or grandness, was not attractive, was despised by his peers, misunderstood, made fun of and was not considered to be anyone's hero, except for twelve disciples he had chosen to be his friends. Most of them were challenged in some way and in need of a teacher who could instruct and inspire them to reach their full potential, as disciples and purveyors of the words spoken by Jesus and inspired by God. Most weren't considered "special" in Jewish society. In fact, the tax collector Matthew was hated by the Jews. Simon Peter, Andrew, James and John were uneducated fishermen. Yet their leader Jesus taught them how to become effective servants through suffering and sacrifice. And the religious leaders, their opposition, the other "gang," soon became so angry at the success and popularity of this group that they sought not only to disband them but to have them all killed! Does this sound like a story that could have been written today?

Let's review this chapter together before you begin reading what Mark has to say to his target audience, the youth of today. I have chosen "The Message" version of this scripture because it uses some of the same vernacular as Mark has used in this book and to which youth of today can relate.

Isaiah 53 (*The Message*)

Who believes what we've heard and seen? Who would have thought God's saving power would look like this?
The servant grew up before God - a scrawny seedling,
a scrubby plant in a parched field.
There was nothing attractive about him,
nothing to cause us to take a second look.
He was looked down on and passed over,
a man who suffered, who knew pain firsthand.
One look at him and people turned away.
We looked down on him, thought he was scum.
But the fact is, it was our pains he carried -
our disfigurements, all the things wrong with us.
We thought he brought it on himself,
that God was punishing him for his own failures.

But it was our sins that did that to him,
that ripped and tore and crushed him - our sins!
He took the punishment, and that made us whole.
Through his bruises we get healed.
We're all like sheep who've wandered off and gotten lost.
We've all done our own thing, gone our own way.
And God has piled all our sins, everything we've done wrong,
on him.
He was beaten, he was tortured,
but he didn't say a word.
Like a lamb taken to be slaughtered
and like a sheep being sheared, he took it all in silence.
Justice miscarried, and he was led off -
and did anyone really know what was happening?
He died without a thought for his own welfare,
beaten bloody for the sins of my people.
They buried him with the wicked,
threw him in a grave with a rich man,
Even though he'd never hurt a soul
or said one word that wasn't true.
Still, it's what God had in mind all along,
to crush him with pain.
The plan was that he give himself as an offering for sin
so that he'd see life come from it - life, life, and more life.
And God's plan will deeply prosper through him.
Out of that terrible travail of soul,
he'll see that it's worth it and be glad he did it.
Through what he experienced, my righteous one, my servant,
will make many "righteous ones,"
as he himself carries the burden of their sins.
Therefore I'll reward him extravagantly -
the best of everything, the highest honors -
Because he looked death in the face and didn't flinch,
because he embraced the company of the lowest.
He took on his own shoulders the sin of the many,
he took up the cause of all the black sheep.

Think about this verse as you read and learn from Mark's book.

Never Bully or Judge Anyone

"Bully - a person, who hurts, frightens or tyrannizes over those who are smaller or weaker." Daniel Webster

"Do not let any unwholesome talk come out of your mouths, but only what is helpful for building others up according to their needs, that it may benefit those who listen." Ephesians 4:29 NIV

"When you judge another, you do not define them, you define yourself." Unknown

In this present day and age, people have to be so careful about how they speak and what they say to others. Your words and actions have the power to either edify or destroy people. You can be the "build-up king" by encouraging them and making them feel good and confident about themselves or be the "tear-down bully" by using your words as weapons to hurt and harm someone. It is upsetting when people use their words to deliberately inflict pain. Some people do not think before they speak. They just say whatever they feel and do not think that bullying, spreading hurtful rumors and being critical towards people is a big deal.

You hear it everywhere you go from middle school, high school, college, work and even during activities in everyday life. People are always talking about someone else, saying hurtful and mean things. Individuals do not realize the power of their words. They think that when they talk about someone they are just harming and hurting only the person they are bullying or talking about. Instead they are harming themselves as well, when they say hurtful and critical things about others.

"Do to others as you would have them do to you." Luke 6:31 NIV

When my sister Jenna was in high school, there was a girl named Karen who was always bullying her. She would bully her because Jenna is pretty, smart and a great athlete. Karen was always jealous of her. She always wanted what Jenna had. Karen would make up vicious lies about my sister and spread them around the school and try to make other people hate her. This girl was rude and a bully. My sister would get so upset that she would have to eat lunch in the library because so many people would pick on her because Karen was bullying her and encouraging others to do the same thing. This constant bullying caused my sister to hate school. Her school life became miserable because other students were so mean to her, all because of one bully.

Now, five years later Jenna has become a stronger, more confident person because of the adversity she faced in high school. Even though Jenna could have handled the situation better by confronting her bullies, she was able to overcome the trials and tribulations which built up her character. The effects of bullying do not always turn out as well as they did in Jenna's case. Some kids who are bullied never recover from the trauma. As we have heard so many times in the news, some kids even end up committing suicide over being bullied by other students. How would you feel if someone you knew had attempted suicide or actually killed themselves because of a thoughtless word you spoke or something mean you had done to them? In the cases of these kids, you hear about who perpetrated the bullying that lead to someone committing suicide, can you imagine living with the guilt of that for the rest of your life? Think about it. Don't become a "victim" of bullying in either way. Confront bullying when it happens to you and do not bully others either, because you never know how someone will react to your callous or thoughtless actions. It is a scar that so many youth of today will eventually wish they had never inflicted on another person.

The lessons I learned from seeing how Jenna handled this situation were two-fold. First, don't ever allow bullying to control your life and actions. Stand up for yourself. Seek help from those in authority. Don't be afraid to call-out your bullies. Expose them for who they are. Furthermore, I would never want to face the guilt of my negative actions on another person's life. It's just not worth it. A moment of hatred or "just poking fun at someone" could change their whole life and your life as well, because of the burden of guilt. It's a conscious choice and the right choice!

Some kids and young adults just don't get it that it is not okay to bully someone, and there are negative consequences that come along with it. If you bully someone and say hurtful, mean and nasty things such as, "you are ugly," "nobody likes you," or on a more serious note, "Nobody cares if you're alive. You're a waste of life." How do you think that makes the other person feel? Whether you pick on them and say it right to their face or by cyber-bullying, what do you think that does to the person you are picking on and bullying? It probably does not make them feel too good about themselves. In fact, it probably makes them feel terrible because you made a nasty remark about them. Turn it around. If you were that person that you were picking on, would you like it? Or better yet, how would it make you feel? All people need to feel cared about, accepted, respected and loved.

I remember when I was in middle school, in 6th grade, these kids were bullying my friend Keith. Two kids ganged up on him, laughing at him, picking on him and trying to push him around. One of our best friends Jimmy was a really big kid. He must have been 6'0" in 7th grade. Jimmy saw them picking on Keith when he was walking out of gym class, and I will never forget how he took both kids that were picking on Keith, grabbed one up in each arm and pinned them up against the lockers and said, "I suggest that you never pick on my friends or anyone else in this school. You got it?"

From another perspective, what if those bullies picked on another person in my school who was really going through a tough time in life? Before you judge, pick on and bully someone else, first try to imagine yourself in their place. You have no idea why some people act the way they do. You can only see outside appearances such as how they look and act. You cannot see the true feelings and intentions of their hearts. Some people have so many deep cuts and scars on the inside, and the very last thing they need is for someone to start picking on them, bullying them, telling them what a worthless person they are and spreading rumors that are not true.

Never look down on anybody. You hear people all the time whether it is at school, work, wherever it may be, people will say, "I can't believe they look or act like that." Before you go over and pick on them and say anything negative about them, you first need to go take a long walk in their shoes.

One time I was getting ready to go train for hockey at the rink, and I showed up early. I thought my practice was at 11:00am, but it wasn't until 12:45pm. So, I went across the street to a small diner and found a vacant barstool. I sat down next to a man about 55 years old. He looked very poor and run down. I smiled at him and said, "Hello, how are you?" He answered back gruffly, "I was doing okay until you came around and asked me how I was. Nobody has taken the time to give me a smile and ask how I was doing in quite awhile." We continued talking for a while, and the stories he was telling me about himself were things that were, in fact, heartbreaking. He told me he had a good job, got fired, began to take out his frustration on his family and was now homeless. Despite his many problems, he seemed to be a genuinely nice guy. I noticed that he was very polite to the woman taking his order.

I thought about how many times we encounter people like this guy and how we either just ignore him or think, "What is wrong with that guy? Why does he dress so strangely and look so scruffy?" You have to remember that if you are always bullying, judging, being critical and harsh towards people, you better get ready because whatever you give, you're going to get back. Never look down on anybody and make them feel insecure. Build them up and help them feel good about themselves.

A lesson that I have learned is to always give people encouragement and hope. There are plenty of people who bully and harass others in our world today. The last thing anyone needs is for someone to come along, bring them down by pointing out their weaknesses and rejecting them. Instead of bullying that person and bringing them down, build them up and put encouragement in their heart. Matthew Chapter 7 talks about entering through the narrow gate. Most people choose the wide gate. Sometimes that is not the best way to go. Even if it means being different than everyone else and sticking up for that person, it's the right thing to do. Be there to build people up, don't knock them down, judge and pick on them.

ACTION PLAN:

Take a moment today and think, have you ever bullied someone, picked on someone or started a rumor about someone? Think about how you would feel if it was the other way around. How would you feel if someone was bullying you and spreading rumors about you? If you are doing that today, stop it! If you did that in the past, go to that person, apologize and say that you are sorry, and you realize that you hurt them. If you see someone else being a bully or spreading rumors, be the person that sticks up for the person being bullied. Be the bigger person. It's easy to laugh and joke about them, but be bold and stand up for what is right!

Enjoy Life. It's Short.

"Teach us to number our days, that we may gain a heart of wisdom." Psalm 90:12 NIV

"Life is what we make it, always has been, always will be."
Grandma Moses (Renowned American Folk Artist)

Life is short, period. There are only 86,400 seconds, 1440 minutes, or 24 hours in one day (8 hours of which most people sleep.) So that only leaves 16 hours a day. Many people get so focused on their own goals and dreams that they forget the simple and best things that they should be enjoying the most which is their family and the people that they love!

Life is a journey not a guided tour. There is always another challenge to face once we accomplish our current goal. Then another goal replaces that one in your heart and so on. If we live just for the destination and not the journey, we will look up one day and regret that we totally missed out one of the most important parts of life - our family and the people that we love. You have to remember and never forget that family ends in *ily*, which stands for "*I love you*."

So how can you get the most blessings from and for your family? Put God #1 in your life, and He will set your priorities! He will teach you what is really important as primary in your life. Joel Osteen, Pastor of Lakewood Church in Houston, once said "You have an opportunity to leave a mark that cannot be erased." If you apply this principle to your relationship with your family by making them a top priority, you'll leave them something that will last forever.

Many people become so focused and caught up on their career, social activities and goals that their life goes by in the blink of an eye.

Matthew 16:26 says: ***"What good will it be for a man if he gains the whole world, yet forfeits his soul?"***

In other words, "What can a man give in exchange for his soul?" Like losing your soul, losing your family, while getting caught-up in the world, is another cherished relationship in life you don't want to sacrifice.

Some people spend a lifetime trying to accomplish and reach their personal goals, leaving little or no time for anything else, especially their families. Although their achievements may be great, it's a hollow victory. Once they reach their goals, the enduring satisfaction they'd hoped to achieve is short-lived, and the cost they paid by neglecting their family is overwhelming! When you hang out with your family at home, have dinners together, go on vacations or go on adventures, those things make memories to last a lifetime. It's about being with your family and the people that you love, and doing the simple things in life that bring out the best in life and encourage true happiness.

My parents would always do simple things that had a huge impact on my sisters and me. They would both write notes on our lunch bag napkins, saying, "We love you; we are proud of you; keep going; you are awesome!" - Love, Mom and Dad. That is something so simple yet profound. Simple, thoughtful actions teach us the valuable lesson that life is way too short, and you need to tell your family all the time how much you love them and that you are proud of them.

A friend's father found out he had cancer. The doctors told him he only had a few months to live, there was nothing else that they could do and everything was on God's timetable. Some people would get depressed and discouraged; however, my friend's dad had faith. So, his family and friends had a fundraising party for him, and he remained really positive, happy and upbeat. While at the fundraiser, I overheard an older gentlemen asking the father what his advice was on life. I will never forget what he said. He started off by saying with a deep voice, "Do you hug and kiss your family every day you can and give them a high five and tell them "good job" and that you love them? If someone you really care about and love only had a few months to live, how would you treat them? Never take a single day for granted. Appreciate and cherish the moments that you have together. Every day is a valuable gift and blessing from God. You don't know how long you will live or what God's timetable is for someone you love. Tell your family and friends that you love them and that you are so happy to have them in your life. Tell them all the time. You can never tell them enough; life is too short. Those words planted a seed in my heart, and it is something that I will never forget. I believe it was a powerful life lesson that will be remembered by those who heard him say it.

My friend Carl was a top football player. He holds several records at his high school for receiving yards as a wide receiver. He was ranked among the top 5 receivers in the state. The football team had a big game coming up to qualify for the state championship game, and he was a big part of the game plan. He was a very determined young man, and several colleges were after him to offer him a scholarship for football and academics. Two days before the state championship qualifying game, he had to tell his coach that he couldn't make it to the game. He said that his father was getting honored at a firefighters' dinner for rescuing a young lady that was in a raging fire, and he wanted to be a part of that celebration and honor for his father. He went on to tell the coach that his father wanted him to go to his game, and his father would be really disappointed if he missed the game. However, Carl knew that his father was always at his games, having never missed a game in the past. He was always supportive and cheering him on. This was Carl's chance to return the favor and dedication to his father by being there for him. His father was very important to him, and this was Carl's way of showing him.

Or it can be the total opposite. It can be a parent who doesn't have his priorities straight. I was working with my Dad, and we were on a jobsite, and I was standing talking to my Dad and Sam, a scrap steel owner. "Scrapper Sam" had a very successful business. I learned something from him that I will never forget. He had made it to the top in his field. He was the top scrapper in the New York area, yet he did it at the expense of time with his family. I can remember as I was standing there that day, his cell phone rang, and it was his son. I could hear his son on the other end of the line because his phone speaker was so loud. He said, "Dad, you will never guess, my school team made it to the semi-final lacrosse championship game. I want you to come!" You could tell the kid was so excited. The kid went on to say, "Dad, I know you are busy at work and never come to any of my games, but I would really like it if you came and watched me and our team!" Sam answered his son, "James, I am sorry I am too busy at work, trying to get all these drivers out and on the road. I won't be able to make it." I thought to myself, "That kid is so excited for his lacrosse team and wants his Dad to go so bad, and he is not going." What I learned from the decision Scrapper Sam made that day was even though he was considered a top scrapper when it comes to scrap metal, he had "scrapped" the most important part of his life, his family. He wasn't making them his top priority.

Your family deserves more than you just saying, "Sorry, I can't go tonight," or "I can't make it; I am too busy." In other words you are saying that work or what you are doing during that time is more important than your family; work is first or your agenda is first, and your family is second. You have to remember in life there are some things you won't ever be able to get back. There are no "re-do's." Don't be so busy with your life or obsessed with your job that you can't go to your family's sporting events, concerts or a special occasion, whatever the case may be.

Just like my parents have encouraged me, your family needs to know that you love and support them in anything they do and that you are proud of them. Slow down and enjoy the little things in life. That's what life is all about. So many people are too focused and too busy to the point where they are totally missing out on the best things in life, which are their families. Appreciate them! Love the people that God has brought into your life.

Action Plan:

Cherish your family whether it's your parents, siblings, grandparents, aunts, uncles or cousins. Even if you do not have a family or a family that is close by, form a 'family relationship' with some very close friends and treat them in a similar manner. Go tell them how much you appreciate them in your life and how much you care about them, support them and how much you love them. If you make God your "#1 Priority," He will help you get the most out of the "2nd Most Important Priority," your family which will heap blessings on you and them. Then, everything else will fall into place. Remember, family ends in *ily* - *I love you*.

Love Others and Yourself.

"A new command I give you: Love one another. As I have loved you, so you must love one another. By this all men will know that you are my disciples, if you love one another."

John 13:34-35 NIV

"What you think about yourself is much more important than what others think of you." Marcus Annaeus Seneca (Roman Rhetorician and Writer, ca. 54 BC - ca. 39 AD)

You have to love yourself and have confidence in yourself. So many people compare themselves to everybody else that they admire. Too many of us get obsessed with other people's blessings. Be confident in the person you are and be thankful to God for your personal blessings. People can get so caught up in competing to see 'who's the best' that they may not reveal who they really are. Just be yourself.

Too many people are ashamed of themselves, and it shows. The way you carry yourself is sending out a big message about you to others. People are going to treat you according to how you present yourself. Carry yourself with confidence and pride. You might be worried and afraid of what others will think of you instead of concentrating on being the unique person you are. Love and respect yourself! One thing that you can never do is leave yourself. You can leave friends and people that are being mean to you, or you don't want to be around, but you can never leave yourself. You can never walk away from you. God breathed his life into you and made you. He wouldn't have made you if He didn't want you to reveal the person you truly are. Be proud of who you are and what makes you, you! You are special, so love yourself and never give up on you!

We've all heard the slang saying, "God didn't make no junk!" All that He has made is for good, when we seek Him in all we do. Remember, just be YOU and love yourself. You are valuable and have so much potential in you waiting to be expressed. Search deep inside yourself, and you will see it! YOU are unique and one of a kind!

Action Plan:

Are you being the person that God created you to be? Can you love and accept this person? Remember God knew your actions, and what you were going to be like long before you were born. Make a list of the qualities you like best about yourself. Just for starters, are you friendly, kind, smart, hard-working and/or thoughtful? Now think about the qualities others have told you they like about you. Take that list and read it to yourself every day and memorize it. As you think of other qualities, add them to the list.

Be A True Friend.

"The wise prevail through great power, and those who have knowledge muster their strength." Proverbs 24:5 NIV

"A friend is one who believes in you when you have ceased to believe in yourself." Unknown

More often than not, people will only socialize and be friends with people that are just like them. We are naturally attracted to people who are a lot like ourselves; have the same passions, personality types and common interests. The reason for that is because it is so simple and comfortable to fit in and associate with similar people.

What about the people that are the opposite of us that we call "different", the groups and people that don't have the same passions and interests as us? You've probably heard someone say, "I am not going to get along and be friends with that guy, just look at him!" or "That guy looks mean and he's been in trouble with the law." That doesn't give you the right to treat them like they are inferior. What I have learned is that you should get to know that person before passing any judgment. Some of the most generous people are the ones with noticeable problems and hang-ups. To be honest, you might be able to trust that person that you call "different" a lot more than you can trust your "group of friends." Many people don't know the reasons why people have the hang-ups they have. You should always try to be more understanding towards others.

When I was in high school, there would always be the stereotypical groups of the "athletes", the "smart ones", the "preps" and the "different" ones. I always asked myself, "Well, what is different? What makes you different?" People need to get over the "doesn't measure up to my standards" attitude. I remember times when some people would say right out loud, "As long as you act like me, have the same passions and interests as me, then I will like you, get along with you and be friends with you." It's almost like you had to pass a test to become someone's friend.

I learned that, nowadays, too many people don't choose their friends for the sake of friendship. My parents taught me from an early age not to choose my friends because they were the star athlete of the school or because they were popular, the class clown or the pretty girl that everybody likes. They told me to choose my friends because they are kind, caring, and you just enjoy being around them. Today, I understand more than ever what my parents were teaching me. They weren't saying to be friends with every single person you come in contact with but at least be sincere and generous to everybody that crosses your path. My mom would always tell me when I was in school, "If you see anybody sitting at a lunch table alone, go sit with them and make new friends, better yet, invite them to sit with you and your group. You never know the impact you will have on someone else."

For example, my senior year of high school, something happened that totally changed my heart. I was taking a class required for graduation. The teacher never took sides, and she always seemed to understand where people were coming from with their thoughts and ideas. It was the first day of class, and she had us play a game called the line game. The whole class stood on the line, and she would ask questions such as do you live in a house, do you have a car, do you have siblings, questions like that. A question that stood out was this particular one. She asked, "Does anybody feel lonely or ever feel like they have no friends and feel like they are just aren't good enough?" One kid was bold and had enough faith to step over that line. My heart instantly went to my stomach. I felt so badly for him and was upset emotionally.

Later I noticed that he had the same lunch time as me. One day, I saw him sitting all by himself at the corner lunch table where nobody could see him, so I went over and sat by him. He was very quiet and shy. I introduced myself and just asked him to tell me about himself.

He told me his name was Ricky and that he just moved to our city because his workplace is right by the school and his apartment. He went on to tell me that he had experienced a very rough life. He moved out of his house because his father was an alcoholic and drug addict, subject to angry rages and violence. He went on to say that his mother passed away when he was in first grade.

His life was very difficult. His dad would come home at night drugged up and would physically and mentally abuse him. You could tell that he was struggling and on his own, because he only had three shirts and wore the same pajama pants almost every day. He told me that he worked every single day, and this was his daily schedule: he would come to school at 7:45 am until school was over at 2:30 pm, then he would go home, do homework, sleep for a little bit, then work at his job from 11 pm until 7:00 am in the morning, then he would head off back to school. His story made me feel very sad for him.

After sharing all this with me, he opened a red notebook and began to draw. I couldn't believe my eyes when I saw his amazing drawings. I even asked him if he traced them, and he replied, "No,

I drew them myself." I saw incredible drawings of a portrait of a person, of animals, of a window and the sky beyond. I asked him if I could see the rest of his drawings, because they were so good, and I was impressed. He gave me his notebook, and as I was flipping through it, I came across a poem. The title of his poem was "Nobody Will Miss Me." The poem's main point was that people would always judge him, laugh at him, and, in fact, even beat him up for no reason at all except for being "different." I was so heartbroken; I gave him my cell phone number and said, "You have a friend in me, in fact, a true friend... I promise." Suddenly, Ricky smiled the biggest smile, and in an appreciative voice, said "Thank you!"

The next day in the classroom, he handed me his notebook and said, "Read this, I have written a poem for you." It was a poem and a picture that he had drawn. The poem read:

"My New Friend"

"I finally found and have a friend, someone that actually cares about me and took the time to reach out to me. I know he has my back, and he is a true friend. He even said you got a friend in me, I promise. I totally believe in him that he is my friend. What Mark doesn't know is the day he talked to me and got to know me for the person I am, I had a loaded gun in my apartment that was ready to go. I was going to pull the trigger when I got home from school. I had the gun in my hand ready to fire, but I kept hearing this kid's voice, heart and seeing him saying, "You are such a talented drawer, and you got a friend in me. I promise." I thought to myself I would hurt my friend way too much if I did this. I set that gun down faster than you can imagine. I am so excited that I will see my friend, in fact, my best friend tomorrow at school. He saved my life because he showed interest in me.

Your friend, Ricky."

I thought all I had done was to be friendly and include him, make him know that I cared about him. I wasn't treating him differently than any of my other friends. The little life lesson that I learned is that it makes such a difference in somebody's life when you take the time and get to know someone and hear his or her story. It is so easy to laugh and say, "You don't measure up to my expectations or my friends' criteria." Try to include most everyone you know on your "friends" list. You might not talk to them all the time, but make friends with as many people as you can. Let them know that you care about them. Take the time to find out what makes that person who they are. Some of you would have many more friends, or who knows - maybe even a friend for life! Who are you to judge? Never put someone in the "not my friend" category.

Remember, Proverbs 18:24 says, ***"There are friends who destroy each other, but a real friend sticks closer than a brother."***

Let me ask you, whom are you sticking close to like a brother or sister? I know there are other people like Ricky, someone who needs you to be their friend, someone who could use your acceptance and friendship. Sometimes a desperate person goes to another person as a last resort before they give up hope. You may be the one person that makes an attempt at friendship with someone who is dying of loneliness on the inside. The person you befriend may give life a second chance just like Ricky did. They could be doing the absolute best they can with who they are and what they have. This was certainly true in Ricky's case. Show acceptance to everyone! Never ignore someone that you don't think meets up to your friends' checklist. Expand your friends list. Don't just have a few friends; have a lot of them! It makes life more diverse and interesting.

ACTION PLAN:

This week when you go out whether it's at school, college, work or just anywhere in the real world, notice if you are only associating with people that are "just like you" or measure up to your standards. If that is true, be bold enough and include and get to know somebody with whom you normally wouldn't associate. Make new friends, in fact, maybe that next "somebody" will end up being one of your closest friends. Being friendly might help you and your new friend reach your individual dreams and goals.

Perform Random Acts of Kindness.

"He who is kind to the poor lends to the LORD, and he will reward him for what he has done." Proverbs 19:17 NIV

"Remember there's no such thing as a small act of kindness. Every act creates a ripple with no logical end." Scott Adams (American Satirist & Creator of the *Dilbert* comic strip)

One of the meanings of "Integrity" is to do the right thing when no one else is watching. It's not about being perfect, but as a person, you need to be the real deal. So many people today are praying and hoping for something great to happen to them. Do at least a few good things for someone else every day. It doesn't have to be some big thing, but everyone can do simple, small acts of random kindness. The biggest lesson I remember was when my parents would tell us that we could be exactly what another person needs to keep going in life. If you think about it, giving is the most rewarding and best way to live. Every day, make yourself available to do little acts of kindness for others.

One of the most valuable lessons I learned in Sunday school was when we were taught about how Jesus treated people He met during His short ministry on earth. He always would greet people in respect to the circumstances they were in at the time. If they needed a friend, He became their friend. If they were hungry, He fed them. If they were in need of spiritual guidance, He ministered to that need. The main point of the lesson for that week was basically telling us wherever Jesus went, He was good to people, freely dispensing hope and joy to everyone in need. In Jesus' own words ***"Do ye likewise."*** You should go out and try to do the same thing. Help everyone you can who has a need. If they are having tough times, comfort them with your compassion and willingness to help.

One time I went with another family to a women and children's shelter. It was a refuge where women and their children could go if they were abused or homeless. The shelter's program helped them get their lives back on track and gave them hope for a brighter and better future.

It was Christmas Eve, and we were serving dinner to them. At one of the tables, I asked a little kid named Max what he would like for Christmas. He said in a hopeful voice, "I wish Santa would bring me a toy helicopter." Then his mother replied, "I know you asked Santa for it, but if he doesn't bring you a helicopter, don't be mad at Santa." In other words she was saying, "I can't afford that, Max." After hearing that, I simply took action and made sure that Max's Christmas wish would come true. The next morning Max woke up to a brand new toy helicopter! It really didn't take much to make two people very happy that Christmas!

I thought about how many times people have felt compassion in their hearts to do an act of random kindness, and then they reconsider and say, "I can't do this right now, maybe next time." Never miss an opportunity to do an act of random kindness and be the answer to someone's prayer. Often people ignore opportunities to be kind. Deep down in their heart, they know that person needs love or compassion from someone. Only you can make the decision to be that someone.

If you ever see someone down on themselves, talking negatively, acting discouraged, and not behaving like they normally would, it's easy to just walk by and ignore them. If you see that situation happening, go over to that person and say something encouraging. Help them out by giving them some advice or guidance in the right direction. Sometimes, just a few kind words can go a long way in helping that person.

I recall another memorable act of kindness happened one day while I was watching a TV show. It provided another life lesson for me. The television program featured a certain company that had done something for a family that was less fortunate. The family needed to dig up a pipe in their backyard because it was clogging up their sewer, and they couldn't afford to pay for this service. The company told them that they would bring over an excavator and dig up the yard, so they could locate and fix their pipe. It was a long process helping them clean up, remodel and renovate. When the company finished the job, the family asked how much they owed. The generous owner told them, "Nothing. Put it towards other needs your family might have. They deserve it."

Sometimes all people need is your time. People always ask, "How do you change the world to make it a better place?" I believe the answer is doing at least one act of random kindness every day. It could be something as simple as volunteering your time to a worthy cause or donating to a favorite charity. A simple act of kindness may be giving a homeless man a care pack containing everyday necessities that we take for granted. If you are crossing the bridge, and there is a toll, pay it for the person behind you.

Look around for creative ways to do acts of random kindness. It's easy to do things for the people that will pay us back and reward us, but what about the people that can't do anything at all for you? Or maybe you spot someone you know is having a tough time, struggling to get by. Try giving them a gift card to a restaurant or grocery store or a personal gift you have picked out yourself. Just a simple act like that could help them realize someone cares and could encourage their hearts until their circumstances change.

Instead of viewing interruptions as inconveniences, see them as opportunities. You never know, you could be exactly what they needed. Who knows? Maybe you are their lifesaver. You are the one who can make a big difference! Your goal should be to do at least one act of random kindness each day.

ACTION PLAN:

Today, reach out to someone who may need a helping hand or someone who needs you to listen to them. You will find out that when you give compassion to others, you receive the best and greatest gift of all. Live to give!

Have Faith.

"In Him we were also chosen, having been predestined according to the plan of Him who works out everything in conformity with the purpose of His will, in order that we, who were the first to put our hope in Christ, might be for the praise of His glory."

Ephesians 1:11-12 NIV

"Miracles happen every day." Unknown

My grandparents would say, "Never ponder on something too

long and don't be discouraged about anything for too long, either." God is in complete control. They would go on to say, "When you trust in God, there will be no reason to worry, and you will feel a comfort in your heart." There is enough worry in the world. Don't worry and stress out like the world. Often the reason we become anxious is because we don't have patience. Our goal is taking longer than we hoped, or we don't see an answer to our prayers. If you pray for patience, do you think God gives you patience or the opportunity to become patient? If someone prays for health, do you think God gives them perfect health right away or the opportunity to become healthy?

One of our family friends named Allison has a daughter named Alyssa, who was diagnosed with brain cancer when she was only 7 years old. Today Alyssa is 10 years old, and she is still going strong and fighting the good fight. At first her mother Allison was super sad, always worried and uptight about Alyssa's future. Would she have one? Somehow, during her daughter's treatments, she stepped out in faith which changed her attitude. At first, she lost sleep many nights worrying about her daughter and could have easily given up and said, "God, why my daughter?" However, she had faith. Allison often talked about how God is always working His magic in our lives. She didn't get discouraged just because she didn't see anything happening. When Allison saw her daughter going through treatment after treatment, she would say in faith, "God is working."

Allison's faith taught me a lesson that God is working even when we don't see any evidence of it. I'm sure that all of you can look back at a time in your life when you didn't see anything happening, but you kept on believing, and that time was the truest test of your faith. How many times have you been thinking about someone, and then you randomly see that person at the store, or they call you? That isn't random and out of the blue. That is God letting you know that He cares about everyone and everything in your life. At times you know without a doubt, when you can look back on your life that God was working during hard times, as well as the good times. Quit asking why nothing good ever happens to you. God is beside you fighting every battle and setting up the good things that happen in your life as well.

For example, I was recently in Orlando, Florida, attending a "Night of Hope" event lead by Joel Osteen, Pastor of Lakewood Church in Houston. There were thousands of people in attendance. I was waiting for Pastor Osteen to start his program, and I literally bumped into a successful Christian businessman, Craig Keeland, who introduced himself to me. We were having a pleasant casual conversation, and when the conversation turned to me, I told Craig I was writing a book, and he responded by showing a genuine interest in my story. Then he began to share with me his own book writing experiences, which eventually led me to contact Terry Minke at CIS Publishing, the company that helped me publish this book. I'm sure you can look back in your life and see how you've experienced similar events in your life. That is not luck! That is meant to be! Step by step, God is with you all the way. He is creating events in your life that will help you get to that next level. Stop worrying about everything and just enjoy your life. You may not see His hand of favor right now, but you can learn to trust Him. Psalm 91:2 boldly proclaims, ***"I will say of the LORD, He is my refuge and my fortress, my God, in whom I trust."*** That is saying when you trust the Lord with all of your heart, everything will be fine. Don't get frustrated and start complaining because nothing is happening according to your plan or on your timetable. If you just have faith and trust, then you will enjoy your life a lot more.

ACTION PLAN:

Maybe today you're not facing anything as serious as Alyssa.

Still, you need to know that God has complete control of your life and is directing you. We all have difficulties in life that can make us anxious and steal our joy. But, you need to turn all those worries, fears and sadness over to God and trust Him. Expect good things and have faith, knowing that God is in control.

Don't Judge by Outward Appearances.

"Stop judging by mere appearances, but instead judge correctly." John 7:24 NIV

"All stereotypes turn out to be true. This is a horrifying thing about life. All those things you fought against as a youth: you begin to realize they're stereotypes because they're true." Unknown

Take notice sometime how some people won't accept other people that are not like themselves. If they aren't the same skin color or nationality or have different job descriptions or religious backgrounds, they will most likely not associate with them. You have to remember, we all have the same Creator. Your prejudice based on these criteria can set a huge barrier between you and them. I believe that the world would be a much better place if people would accept others who are different than themselves and have more respect for those people 'beyond the barrier.' Some people need to learn to get rid of the assumptions and stereotypes they have about others. Most of the time that judgmental attitude is based on a deep-seated prejudice.

I can remember a time when my friend and I were in gym class one day, and I mean this with all respect, one kid in our class was black. After we got out of gym class, one kid reported that his locker was broken into, and his phone and money were missing.

Another kid in the locker room came over and said, "Just blame the black kid and check his locker. I bet he stole it." My friend Jeff immediately came to the black kid's defense saying, "That kid is the nicest kid in the world. To be honest, he would be the last kid we would have to worry about stealing anything!"

Some people get so caught up in prejudging and assuming that certain people are bad news because of their appearance or their family background. Too many times people will prejudge without even getting to know you or that other person. This was exactly how those students in the locker room were quick to prejudge the black kid just because he was black and, by doing so, stereotyped him for his skin color.

John 3:16 says ***"For God so loved the world that He gave His one and only Son, that whoever believes in Him shall not perish but have eternal life."***

That is saying that God loves the world. He loves the whole world! He doesn't only love a certain group. He loves everybody.

One time my family and I had checked in at the airport for the flight home from a vacation in Florida. The rest of my family got Row 4, and I got stuck with Row 11. My parents and sister boarded the plane and sat together. They tried to save the seat across from them, so I could at least sit close by them, but someone took that seat. So I was sitting about seven rows back, and a man from the Middle East came and sat right next to me. He politely said, "Hello, how are you?" To be honest and respectful, I was very uneasy about sitting next to this gentleman. I was prejudging and stereotyping him because of 911 and his appearance. The same thoughts were probably going through both of our heads, "Oh man, this guy must be up to no good; he has something up his sleeve." I decided not to converse with him, and I started reading a magazine that I bought at the airport, yet, despite my obvious disinterest, he began talking to me. He said, "If you go to page 20 and read the article, you'll find it very interesting." Again, I thought, "It's probably a terrible story and something that I don't want to read." But as I started reading, I discovered it was a business article about stocks that are doing well and not so well. He then began talking to me about it, and it was obvious that he wanted to continue our conversation. So I began to talk to him, found out his name was Akil, and the more I talked to him, the more comfortable I felt. I ended up talking to him as if he were my long-lost best friend that I haven't seen in years. We talked about stocks, where he lived, his career and his interests.

After we got to know each other better, he told me that he could tell I was uneasy about sitting next to him and seemed a little uncomfortable even though I had not disrespected him in any way. Later in the conversation, he told me about one time when he was at the airport waiting for his connecting flight, he overheard a conversation between a father and his young son. The father thought that Akil couldn't hear him. The father said, "See that man sitting over there? People like him are people that you can never trust! They are up to no good, and they will hurt you."

While Akil was telling me that story, you could tell it really bothered him. I could detect some anger when he said, "How would they know? That is not true at all about me or my family. Twenty-five family members, including my parents, siblings and our children came to America to better our lives and never intended on hurting or harming other people. Actually, we were fleeing from that type of persecution in the country we came from." It is something that I will never forget.

Don't get caught up by skin color, race or nationality. You can't know somebody by just looking at their outward appearance. The way you know somebody is when you take time to get to know that person and find out what they are all about. Just like you don't judge a book by its cover, first read a few chapters in someone's life. Get to know the person and find out who they are. Life is way too short to live with that type of prejudice. Before you judge someone by their outward appearance, dismiss any prejudicial thoughts about someone, get to know them first, then show them respect once you know who they are on the inside.

ACTION PLAN:

Today, go, reach out and be a friend to someone outside of your group or comfort zone. Instead of doing the normal thing and judging someone in 10 seconds, get to know that person before you judge and make assumptions about them. Could it be that most people act like I did when I first saw Akil on the airplane? I prejudged him and assumed that he was someone I wouldn't like. Today, make a conscious effort to assume the best about someone you encounter that appears to be different than you.

Never Give Up.

"Though a righteous man falls seven times, he rises again." Proverbs 24:16 NAS

"Perseverance is the hard work you do after you get tired of doing the hard work you already did." Newt Gingrich (Former Speaker of the House & Presidential Candidate)

A lesson I learned early in life regarding success and achievement is this. Regardless of what your dreams and goals may be, from an athlete, business executive, politician, teacher to a coach, you have to know that no matter what hardships come along the way or obstacles that you face, you can never give up! You need to keep going and persevere until you achieve your heart-felt goals.

The people that achieve their goals are not always the most skilled, the most intelligent or the most talented. However, they are focused on the task at hand. When they miss the mark or fail, they don't just stay down and out. They don't feel sorry for themselves and see defeat as permanent and give up. They put on their boxing gloves and fight the obstacles they are facing until they win! In other words, there are always going to be heartaches and letdowns that come against you in this life. It's your reaction to them that shapes your future.

In the words of Lance Armstrong, 7-time Tour de France Champion, "Pain is temporary, quitting lasts forever.' Nothing is big enough to destroy your dreams and keep you down and discouraged. God never told anyone when the going gets tough to just give up and throw in the towel. He said a man may fall seven times, yet he gets back up and goes forward. That is such a powerful Word! When you look inside yourself, there is boldness, perseverance and stamina. Just like bikers must have endurance to keep pedaling while cycling uphill, you need to have physical stamina and mental toughness to keep you pushing forward - toward your dreams. You must have the strength to endure and knock down every obstacle in your way. Sometimes you just have to roll with the punches in life, but don't stay down and out. No matter how hard it gets or how badly you want to give up, you cannot give up on yourself. Never let anything come between you and the goals and dreams in your heart. If things get too tough, ask God for help. My publisher shared a quote he remembers hearing his high school coach say all the time, "When the going gets tough, the tough get going!"

Unfortunately, some people will try to keep you down and try to convince and make you believe that you are not good enough or that your goal is too difficult for you. Discouragement can come from a coach, a teacher or maybe someone who is flat-out jealous of you and wants to hold you back. You can't give up on your dreams because you didn't make the cut or win the competition. Maybe you tried and failed. Some people give up on themselves because they think their goal has taken way longer than they thought it should. You have to keep pressing forward and pursuing your dreams. Sometimes you have to get up, brush yourself off, wipe the sweat off your face and keep moving forward and fighting through it. Press on toward achieving your dreams and goals.

I was reading an article about Babe Ruth, one of the best baseball players of all time. Babe Ruth hit 714 home runs in his career and held the record for several decades. Along with that long-standing record number of home runs, however, came a lot of strikeouts... 1,330 to be exact! During his career he also held the record for strikeouts. When he was asked about home runs and strikeouts he said "Every strike brings me closer to the next home run." He never gave up; he just kept trying and trying. Reading that article about Babe Ruth taught me a lesson that tough times were never put in our lives to discourage and defeat us. They are put there to make you stronger! Don't complain and get so upset and discouraged that you give up and quit. Babe Ruth never quit, he just kept swinging away. Anyone can give up and feel sorry for themselves; that's the easy thing to do. Don't let life's obstacles become stumbling blocks. Get up, keep going and remember,

"God is our refuge and strength, a very present help in trouble."
Psalm 46:1.

Never give up on the dreams God has placed in your heart. When it gets tough, and your thoughts say, "Just stop; don't waste any more of your time and energy on this." The harder it gets and the closer you are to giving up, the closer you are to achieving your goal! Develop strength and perseverance deep down in yourself. There are plenty of professional athletes, singers, businessmen and women that could have just given up, but they never abandoned their dreams. They just believed in themselves, prayed and did their best. Never ever give up or at least not too quickly; you never know when big things might be just around the corner. Remember, you have something great in you! You can accomplish anything that God has in His plan for your life as long as you are willing to work hard, put the time into it, and keep the faith.

ACTION PLAN:

Today, take a look around and notice people in your world who are beating the odds and winning the battle, people who are achieving great success! Remember that if God has put dreams in your heart; He will help you achieve them. Dedicate yourself to putting 100% effort into achieving your goals. The sky is the limit; never give up on your dreams prematurely. If you get discouraged and feel like giving up, just say, "I can do this a couple more times." With God's help, you will get there!

Be Happy; Today is Today.

"This is the day the LORD has made; let us rejoice and be glad in it." Psalm 118:24 NAS

"Today is life - the only life you are sure of. Make the most of today." Dale Carnegie (America's Foremost Motivational and Inspirational Author & Speaker)

Your attitude in life is definitely a choice, and you decide every day whether you want to be happy and outgoing or crabby and mad at the world. You must make a commitment to yourself to get the most out of each day by staying focused on the positive rather than the negative. For example, instead of being unhappy about your job because it is boring or unfulfilling, be happy that you have a job at all and do everything you can to do well at it while planning to improve your prospects for a new more exciting one.

My dad has a co-worker who always seemed to be "on-edge" about everything. Whenever I was around him it just seemed as though his negative attitude would start to affect my attitude. I tried at times to interject some positives into our conversations but it seemed as though he would eventually turn the subject back to the negatives again. I eventually had to avoid him as much as I could without being too unfriendly because I could tell he was the type of person who could eventually change the way I looked at the world and people around me.

Things might not always be a downhill ride in life. Sometimes you have to pedal hard uphill, and that's okay. There is nothing wrong with that. However, never let anyone steal your happiness and excitement about life. If you become irritable and mad at the world, you have willingly let something or someone take your happiness away. You are completely in charge of your attitude. It's your "choice" to be happy or sad.

Many people today are just flat-out negative, grouchy and bitter about life. They have no happiness, and everything is a problem. If that is the case for you, you need to start enjoying life, or if you are always happy about your life, encourage others to be happy and make someone else's day better by blessing them in word or deed.

A lot of people go around more focused on what they don't have instead of what they have, for which they should be thankful.

Life is way too short to be irritable and complaining all the time. Don't get caught up in the bitterness of life where nobody wants to be around you. If that is the case, get the joy back in your life. You should be very friendly, easygoing and enjoyable to be around. If you're not feeling happy, find something that will make you "think" happy thoughts! Every day is a gift from God; you have to go out and live life to the fullest.

Some people let their goals get in the way of being happy. They say, "I am not where I planned to be in life at this age. I planned to be here (imagining they are somewhere else) in life and living in this house and driving this car right now." One person I know is constantly down on themselves and irritable because he didn't get the grade he wanted on a test or assignment. He is constantly worried about his next assignment and what grade he needs to make, or he won't be happy about that either. His happiness is dependent on his grades. No, slow down and enjoy today for today. When God wants to bring all that across your path, He certainly will. Trust God's timing. Live each day with happiness and remember when today is gone, it's gone forever! There are no rewind buttons in life where we can go back to yesterday. When you live grouchy and mad at the world, you have totally wasted that day. Never complain and dwell on what is wrong in your life. Start seeing the good in your life and be thankful for what you have. Enjoy today and every day God has given you, one day at a time. The rest of what you are hoping and believing for will come to you soon!

ACTION PLAN:

Take time to repeat this statement aloud several times today, "Wherever I am, this is the place to begin achieving my goals. The work I do today is shaping my future. I can make a list of the things that I am happy and blessed with and read it every day. I am not going to live another day unhappy, worried and irritable." Live every day with happiness and joy!

Make Others Feel Confident.

"If you see the donkey of someone who hates you fallen down under its load, do not leave it there; be sure you help them with it." Exodus 23:5 NIV

"Never look down on anybody unless you're helping him up." Jesse Jackson (American Civil Rights & Political Activist)

Many people in today's world are only worried about themselves. Attitudes seem to be changing to "It's all about me," or even "Just look at me." Most everyone seems to be more concerned about how they are going to get to the next level in life or where they think they should be, rather than caring enough about others to see their needs. I've witnessed that you will always reach your highest potential if you are willing to help others achieve their goals. It may be something as simple as encouraging someone or giving them a compliment when you think they need it. Saying to someone "Good job" or "Keep up the good work" are little words of encouragement that can go a long way.

These are sometimes the same people who think there is no way they can interrupt the pursuit of their goals in life long enough to help others along the way. They think that other people competing against them will keep working harder, progressing more every day and some day surge ahead of them. We should always seek to brighten someone's day and help them to achieve their goals.

One of my teachers that I will never forget was Mrs. Jones. She was an excellent teacher and truly cared about each one of her students. She never made a student feel like they were under par or that they weren't as smart as others in the class. She treated everyone like they were the valedictorian of the school. She always took time and made sure you understood what she was teaching, and if you didn't, she would help you learn the material until you understood it, not settling for anyone to fail. She always treated her students with respect and dignity. Mrs. Jones imparted so much not only into my life, but into the lives of many others as well. She helped many students with college résumés, job applications and wrote great recommendation letters. She was always there to help her students succeed. That is something I will never forget. Maybe you don't think of yourself as a "teacher," but you should always look for opportunities to "teach" or help other people. Maybe it's by sharing with them something you know, showing them how to do something skillfully, or maybe you can help them by giving them advice and direction. Help others whenever you get the opportunity. It may put them on the right path or remove some stumbling blocks on their roadway of life.

At the golf dome where I go to hit golf balls, I used to see this older gentleman on the course that was always trying so hard but just wasn't getting his swing down. One day, a younger man named Robert, who was a top golfer and had won several tournaments in Europe, was walking by this older gentleman that was struggling to hit the ball. Robert stopped and helped him for at least thirty minutes. He showed him the proper swing and technique to hit the ball correctly. After he was done teaching him technique, he began encouraging this gentleman to keep trying. He took the time out of his busy schedule to help someone. It taught me a valuable lesson. You should always help people to feel confident and achieve their best. That is genuine success!

One of my last day's in gym class during my senior year, there was a kid in our class named Eli, who was mentally challenged. We were playing flag football, and I could tell by his enthusiasm, Eli loved football! I asked the gym teacher to put Eli on my team because I knew that the players on our team would pass the ball to him and help Eli score a touchdown. The gym teacher knew that he couldn't play at our skill level. I mean this respectfully, but Eli was uncoordinated and the whole gym class knew it.

One day during a game, I went over to Jordan, a fellow teammate, and told him to let Eli catch the ball and run with it, and he agreed. While our team was in the huddle, I said, "Eli, get ready, we're going to throw the ball to you on this play." As Eli left the huddle, the huge smile on his face pretty much gave away our game plan. His big grin had innocently signaled the other team that he was getting the ball. You could tell by their body language that everyone on the other team, especially the gym class heroes, was thinking, "Are you kidding us?" I imagined them all thinking, "We can't believe, they are going to try to tie this game that we should win!" Everybody in the gym class knew that Eli really didn't have a chance. We threw him the football, and he had a firm grip on the ball and ran as fast as he could with the biggest smile on his face. One kid on the opposing team named Joe was going to touch Eli and grab his flag to end the game, but he didn't. At first, I wondered why? Then I got it. Joe saw Eli running as fast as he could, trying his absolute best, giving it his all. Joe just didn't have the heart to end Eli's triumphant gallop. Eli even ran the opposite way at first and was headed towards his own end zone, and the gym teacher was yelling at him to turn around. The rest of the team finally caught on and acted like they couldn't catch him and grab his flag. Everyone acted like Eli was the fastest wide receiver to ever play the game. What do you know? Eli kept running and scored a touchdown. By the end of the class, he had scored four times!

Remember to help someone every day. Take the time to give people advice and help others flourish. Inspire others to have faith and confidence. Some people think that a legacy of greatness is leaving behind awards, championships and mostly wealth. You can have all the money in the world, and that's great, but in reality it's better to leave a legacy of faith, hope and helping those in need. Don't be so busy and so focused on yourself that you can't help someone else that interrupts your life. Assist others along the way to reach their highest potential, and you could be the person who made the difference!

ACTION PLAN:

Take a look around today and notice if there are people in your life that you might help achieve their goals. Are you taking that extra time to impart something into their lives that could help and impact them forever? Maybe you are good at a certain sport. Are you taking the time to help them out and train them? Or maybe you excel in a school subject that is a real struggle for someone else. Be an encourager and help and impact as many people as you can! Make a difference! Show someone that you care.

Be a Role Model.

"Let no one despise you for your youth, but set the believers an example in speech, in conduct, in love, in faith, in purity."

I Timothy 4:12 ASV

"People never improve unless they look to some standard or example higher and better than themselves." Tyron Edwards (American Theologian, *New Dictionary of Thoughts*, a book of quotations)

Whether you believe it or not, people are watching you. Whether it's your friends, parents, kids or strangers, people will notice you. People observe how you treat people around you and how you live your life. Your actions always speak much louder than your words. Someone is definitely watching and looking either up to you or down at you. Whether we acknowledge it or not, we are role models, and someone is looking up to us for guidance. When you go out in public every day, no matter where you go, you should always be friendly and kind to others. For many years, I didn't think about how many people were watching my actions. My family and I were at Disney World, in Florida, celebrating my grandmother's 90th birthday. I was pushing my grandma around in a wheelchair. It was Christmas time, and we were looking at all the Christmas decorations in the hotel lobby. I was talking to her saying, "Look at the lights. Isn't that neat?" I wasn't doing anything special or unusual. I was just smiling, enjoying the lights and ecstatic to be there with my grandma.

The next day I went down to the hotel salon to see my mom while she was getting her nails done, and a lady that was in the salon with my mother was so happy when she saw me. She said, "I was sitting in the lobby with my husband when you were in the hotel looking at the Christmas decorations and found myself crying happy tears when I saw you pushing your grandma. I could see my son pushing my mother in her wheelchair 5 years ago, just like you were pushing your grandma. You could tell that you were so excited to be with her enjoying the Christmas decorations."

Think about that. Without speaking a word, my actions in the hotel lobby spoke to a stranger who was watching me. I was smiling, showing compassion to my grandma and enjoying the scenery, and someone noticed. Make it your goal to be friendly and compassionate towards the people you encounter every day. Smile and brighten someone's day! Send a friendly message to people with your actions. When you go out into the world, what kind of messages are you sending? Are you kind, friendly and polite to others?

"Similarly, encourage the young men to be self-controlled. In everything set them an example by doing what is good. In your teaching show integrity, seriousness and soundness of speech that cannot be condemned, so that those who oppose you may be ashamed because they have nothing bad to say about us."

Titus 2:6-8 NIV

In other words, be a good role model for others to follow. Do you do this? Do you set a good example for others to follow? Or do you push people away, and are you unpleasant to be around? Are you unfriendly and short-tempered? Things may not always be going right for you in your life, and that is definitely challenging, but you need to find things to be happy about. Remember somebody else in the world always has it worse than you do. There are days that you don't feel like the jolliest person around, but you need to be aware and notice what kind of message you are sending. Don't make a habit of always having a bad day.

I was at the deli shop with my mom one day, and when it was our turn to order, the young guy behind the counter was very curt with his words. "What do you want?" and "Anything else?" I said, "Hello, how are you?" He didn't answer. He wouldn't answer, so I just figured he was having a bad day, and that was okay, I understood. What kind of message do you think he was sending to me? He was basically saying, "Don't bother me." People you encounter won't always have a good attitude, but you need to be a good example regardless of how they act.

The following week when we went back to the deli shop, the girl who usually waits on us took our order. She was smiling and very friendly. We could tell she was happy to serve us. We asked her politely about the guy at the other end of the counter we had encountered on our last visit. She told us that he was always unfriendly and curt with customers. She went on to say that he had no reason to be so negative, that he had everything he could want in life, a great family and a scholarship to college. "He just doesn't like his job," she said.

Are you demonstrating and setting good examples for others to follow? I have learned that you should be a person who puts their best behavior forward as you travel down the road of life. Go out and generously give hope and happiness to others. Be a good role model; people are definitely watching you and could be looking up to you right now. Be a good example.

Action Plan:

Notice and evaluate what message your words and actions are communicating to others. Are you portraying a positive and friendly example? Or are you more like the guy at the deli with the 'don't bother me' attitude? Go out every day with a smile and spread joy to others. Someone needs what you have to share. Determine to be happy and set a good example. People and God are watching you! Be a good role model.

Treat Everyone with Respect.

"Do nothing from selfish ambition or vain conceit, but in humility consider others better than yourselves." Philippians 2:3 NIV

"Never take a person's dignity: it is worth everything to them, and nothing to you." Frank Barron (Former Psychology Professor, University of California Berkeley)

Another life lesson that I learned is to always treat everyone with respect and dignity. I'm sure you've noticed people who only treat others such as the coaches, the teachers or the all-stars on the sports team with respect. There was one person I know who was only nice to others when people he wanted to impress, like teachers, coaches or parents, were present. Otherwise, when they weren't around, he would treat people in a rude and unfriendly manner. However, we need to be kind and friendly to everyone.

Treat everyone with respect. Never stand so tall that you look down upon someone. Some people think that they are "better" than other people and just ignore them. Some people will act like they don't even exist. Don't let that be you! Include everybody. God placed that person in your life for a reason. You may have no idea why. Even if this person can't do anything for you, treat them with respect. You never know. What if someone whose path crossed yours could help you along the way? It could be somebody that doesn't impress you at first glance. You tell yourself, "I don't want their friendship. They can't do anything for me." Take time to be friendly to everyone. How many times do you miss out on an opportunity to be friendly or nice to someone who seems unimportant? Treat everybody like they are a significant person to you!

Here is an example of how you should treat everyone with respect. There was this one class in school that I just couldn't understand. I was always doing poorly on tests and quizzes. One day I told Frank, a fellow classmate, that I was really frustrated and just didn't get it. Frank was one of those students who was very smart and seemed to do well in every subject. He must have had a photographic memory because all he had to do was read the text book, and he could easily recall any part of it. Frank volunteered to tutor me and for some reason when Frank explained what the text was about, I understood it even better than when the teacher taught the same thing. After just three hours of tutoring, Frank prepared me so well that I passed the final exam with flying colors (or letters in this case, since I actually made an A!). You see Frank was someone I probably would not have gotten to know if I hadn't experienced a time of need. Don't miss out and put people in the 'doesn't meet up to my standards' category. Don't say, "I am not going to respect him or her and treat them well because I don't think they help me in any way." As for Frank, I tried to pay him for teaching me the material, as you might pay a tutor, but he wouldn't accept it because he helped me out of the generosity of his heart.

Treat every person the same way you would like to be treated. Remember to say hello, and ask how they are doing. It could be something as simple as smiling at someone or reaching out to a lonely person or greeting and thanking the janitor at school who is cleaning up the hallway after you. Be kind and nice to them.

When I was at school, there was a janitor named Ron that was so quiet, but he was the nicest guy. He reminded me of a big teddy bear. One kid was standing by his locker, with a discouraged look on his face. Ron knew something was wrong, and being the kind-hearted person he was walked over and asked him if anything was wrong. The kid said, "I'm fine. I'm just upset that I didn't get accepted to the college where I wanted to go." Ron asked him what college it was, and the kid told him the name of the school. Ron's face instantly lit up; he smiled and said, "I will put in a good word for you and try my best to get you into that college. You won't believe this, but my brother is the assistant to the Dean."

When you treat people with kindness, it will always come back to bless you! Don't ever overlook the people that cross your path. One or both of you could be holding the right key to the door that will swing open to new opportunities. When you live with this attitude in your heart, it will cause you to treat everyone with respect and dignity. Even if they can't do a thing in the world for you, who cares? Always be good to others, respect them, and show them that they are welcome and appreciated! The Bible tells us to ***"Continue to love each other like brothers and sisters, and remember always to welcome strangers, for by doing this; some people have entertained angels without knowing it."*** Hebrews 13:1-1.

ACTION PLAN:

There will always be times in your life when you cre tempted to ignore people and look down upon them. Never treat others like they are inferior to you. Treat them with respect and dignity. Never overlook the people that come across your path in life. You never know who holds the key to your future! Be kind to everyone!

Just Do It! Who says, "You can't!"?

"Let us not become weary in doing good, for at the proper time we will reap a harvest if we do not give up." Galatians 6:9 NLT

"You just can't beat the person who never gives up."
Babe Ruth (Baseball Hall of Famer)

"I think I can. I think I can. I think I can."
The Little Engine That Could

Many of you have read the story of "*The Tortoise and the Hare.*" In this story, the hare challenged the tortoise to a race. They agreed and raced. The hare thought there was no way that the tortoise could beat him. At first, the hare took off and ran far ahead of the slow moving tortoise. He took his time and lay down and took a nap. All along the way, the tortoise was telling himself, "I can get to the finish line first. I am going to go slow but finish strong." And because he believed that he could, well, you know the rest of the story, the tortoise won the race!

How many times do you tell yourself, "I can't do this."? You think the task and challenges are way too hard. "I can't. I am not good enough, not smart enough and not talented enough." If you say you can't, then, yes you are right; you can't. If instead you say, "I can," it is a totally different story. "I can because I am strong, smart and talented. God has given me gifts." You have to be careful what you say, "I can," or "I can't." There is a big difference! Just like the Tortoise who thought to himself, "I can do this. I might not be the fastest but I am going to get to that finish line! I can do it!"

Every day, you have to tell yourself, out loud and on the inside, "I can do this; I am great; I am talented. I am going to achieve success in life." There's great power in the spoken word. Too many people will tell themselves, "I can't do that. The challenge is way too big, I can't; I am not good enough." If you tell yourself that, who knows? Maybe you are holding yourself back from your highest potential.

Some people have had something happen to them in their past that holds them prisoner in their thought life. Perhaps, you are surrounded by people that make you feel like you are not quite good enough or tell you that you can't do something. Who cares what those negative people think? You have to let that roll off like water on a duck's back. Start telling yourself, "That person told me I can't accomplish my dream or make that team, but I know that I can."

My friend Darin was a very good tennis player. After winning a match, he would tell his opponent, "Man you are such a good player, you can go a long way, keep it up!" Yet he never gave himself credit and never told himself he was a good at tennis and could play well. He would always say, "Well, I can't do this, I have to beat out this guy, and that's too hard." Darin would always make up an excuse and tell himself that he couldn't do something. Maybe you are allowing what someone said about you to hold you back, and that is why you keep telling yourself you can't. It could have been a coach or a teacher.

When I played hockey, there was a coach who always harassed one of the best players on our team. He would say, "You're not talented enough," or "You're not skilled enough." When athletic scouts would come to observe the player, the coach would tell the scouts that he didn't want to put the pressure on the player by having them there during the game and that they would have to come during practice instead. This player determined that he was going to prove that coach wrong. He worked hard and had an 'I can get further than this team' mentality. He proved it, not an arrogant way, but in an 'I can' way. At the end of the season, that player got drafted into a higher league.

Maybe you can relate to that story or maybe not, but the main point is never let someone else's actions or words affect your aspirations. What somebody says about you doesn't matter at all. Let people talk about you all they want. Shrug it off and don't let it keep you from boldly going forward and playing your best. What really matters is where God wants you to be, and He will place you in the right place at the right time.

"I can do all things through Him who strengthens me."
Philippians 4:13 NIV

The Bible verse is saying that when God is with you, all things are possible. There is no task too difficult or too hard for you to accomplish. You must have 'I can do it!' thoughts.

My sister Julie worked out at an athletic club, and there was an overweight man named Chris who was struggling to get back in good shape. People were mocking and telling him, "You can't achieve your weight loss goals. You're too fat!" His so-called friends told him that his goal was unrealistic and impossible. Many of those same friends even convinced him that his lack of physical fitness could affect his eligibility to attend the college of his choice. He allowed those friends to talk him out of following his heartfelt dreams and goals. He settled for the status quo, quit working out at the gym and went to work as a garbage man for a couple years. Later, when my sister encountered Chris back at the gym, she began to faithfully encourage him and tell him that he was talented, very hard-working, and one day he would achieve his goals. Chris took some of Julie's advice to heart and went with it. Today, he has lost a lot of weight and is attending college and majoring in science. Don't let what others say determine whom you will become. Listen for that "still small voice" that will guide you to what's best for you.

Action Plan:

Don't have an 'I can't' attitude. Have an 'I can' attitude! Are people speaking discouragement into your life and preventing you from reaching your best and full potential? You have to be like the tortoise! Slow and steady wins the race! He believed in himself and never let himself be discouraged by the rest of the creatures that were telling him, "You can't win!" He just believed, despite his limitations, and had an 'I can do it' attitude. The next time you are handed a task that you think is beyond your abilities, take a moment and say to yourself, "I think I can." Then start working on the task, taking one little step at a time. Before you know it, you'll have completed this task.

Never Let Criticism Hurt You.

"When pride comes, then comes disgrace, but with humility comes wisdom." Proverbs 11:2 NIV

"Criticism is an indirect form of self-boasting." Emmet Fox (Inspirational Christian Minister and Author of many Christian books in the early 20th century)

Jesus was constantly criticized for always being good to people - helping people in need, healing on the Sabbath and forgiving people's sins. Constant criticism didn't change His mind one bit. He never tried to get revenge on His enemies or explain Himself to them. He just remained focused and determined - just like you should do. We all get criticized.

Sometimes criticism is destructive and is based on jealousy. When you are advancing or excelling in something and someone becomes jealous of you and tries to push and knock you down, that's when you need to stand strong in your convictions. You have a skill or talent, and it is something that they don't have but desire. When you hear untrue criticism about yourself and people start talking badly about you, you don't have to let it affect you. Just stay silent and smile!

Constructive criticism is totally different. That is when someone with good intentions is trying to help us to improve and to achieve our goal. When you receive constructive criticism, remember to thank that person and let them know that you appreciate them for their help and input. I'm sure you can look back and remember people that gave you constructive criticism to help you succeed. It could have been a coach or mentor that was trying to help you improve! My parents taught me at any early age to always be happy for other people when they are succeeding and achieving their dreams and goals. When someone else on your team, at your school, or in the same career as you is advancing and bettering themselves, encourage that person!

When I played hockey, there was this really good hockey player on my spring team. We were at a tournament, a hockey scout noticed his ability, and he actually got drafted that day. I was very upset, discouraged and kind of bitter, and as a result, was mean towards him. I told my parents that I was frustrated with this guy, and the first thing they told me was, "Did you go over to him, give him a handshake and tell him 'good job'?" I just hung my head and said, "No." I had forgotten what they had told me earlier about being happy for someone else's success and achievements. This would become a test of my faith and perseverance. If I stayed jealous of him, then my attitude would impede my personal progress.

I'm sure you can look back and remember a time when you were envious of someone. Don't let jealousy tempt you to start talking negatively about them or pointing out their weaknesses. Rather look at their successes and strengths and, who knows, you may even learn something from them! If you are going to do anything great in your life whether you want to be an athlete, business person, teacher, singer, actress, etc., you have to rise above that negativity and just do what you have to do! In other words "Get the job done and ignore everything else!" Don't take what everybody else is saying so personally.

One summer day, I was playing golf with some friends, and there was a guy named Adam that we caught up to on the course. He started telling us about how he was ranked number 1 and practicing for the challenge to determine the best golfer at the golf course. One day, Adam heard someone talking about him saying, "He's only winning because he is always practicing on the same course, and he gets up early in the morning and goes and hits golf balls at the driving range." So one day, he let that envious person talk him out of going to practice at the golf course which soon changed his routine. He just let that person control his destiny. He let one jealous person that was maybe 30th-50th in the rankings talk him out of being his best! Because of giving in and giving up, to my knowledge, Adam never achieved his goal of being the best on that course. Don't let ANYBODY change the course of your dreams and goals! The more successful you are, the more heat you are going to take from people! Expect opposition, it happens with everything in life! Meet that opposition head-on and become as Joel Osteen would say, "A Champion Within!"

I am sure you have heard this saying many times; "It's better to have tried and failed, than never to have tried at all." Although a wise saying, (even used by Abraham Lincoln in the Gettysburg Address) it's actually a "misquote" from Alfred Lord Tennyson's famous poem *In Memoriam:27, 1850*. Here it what the poem actually says:

Hold it true, whate'er befall;
I feel it, when I sorrow most;
'Tis better to have loved and lost
Than never to have loved at all.

This is great wisdom either way you apply it, and it is a great lead-in to my next chapter on Trust.

ACTION PLAN:

There are always jealous people in your life. They will try to talk you out of your goals and dreams. That is because you have something great that they want and don't have. Remember what happened to Adam at the golf course, the guy who let someone talk him out of being his best by listening to negative comments. If you know someone who is progressing to the next level of victory, encourage that person and be happy for him or her! Don't fall into the jealousy trap!

Trust in Yourself and God.

"Trust in the LORD with all your heart and lean not on your own understanding; in all your ways acknowledge him, and he will make your paths straight." Proverbs 3:5-6 NIV

"No matter how steep the mountain - the Lord is going to climb it with you." Helen Steiner Rice (America's "Poet Laureate of Inspirational Verses")

We all face heartaches at times during our lives. It doesn't matter how happy and generous you are or how much faith you have, you will eventually encounter something or someone that is going to attack your faith and try to destroy it. When that happens, you need to stay strong. It's just like when you workout. The more you lift weights, the stronger you get and your muscle mass increases. Faith works the same way. The more you exercise it, the stronger it gets! Maybe someone you loved passed away. Perhaps a family member or a friend disappointed or hurt you. And on a more personal level, sometimes a serious illness may come against you and attack your faith. However, you have to play with the hand you are dealt from life's deck of cards. It may not make sense to you at all. But, always know that God would have not have allowed it to happen if He didn't have a plan to help you overcome it. If you trust completely in Him, He never gives you more than you can handle.

Losses, failures and disappointments will happen in this life, and they can be very discouraging. Whatever the setback, don't let it stop you from playing your best game in life. With God's help, you can let go of the past. If you are stuck reliving the past and what happened, or what is currently happening to you, you need to have enough faith to accept that and move on. Don't play the blame game. If you need to forgive someone or yourself, make a conscious decision to forgive. This simple act of obedience will transform your life.

Just know and trust that God has your best interests at heart. Sometimes it doesn't matter how hard or long we pray or stand strong in faith, our expectations don't always happen within our time frame. But God hears you. You've just got to believe He can make it happen.

A friend of mine named Rex once told me that he and his mother hadn't spoken to one another for about 6 years. I thought to myself, "Six years is a long time!" Rex was always getting in fights on the street and in school and was always in trouble with the law. And to make matters worse, he was failing in school. I later learned that somehow, Rex got back in touch with his mother after all those years, and with his mother's influence in his life and encouragement for him, Rex has completely turned his act around. Sometimes it just takes faith in someone to make everything work out for the better.

ACTION PLAN:

Always have faith. Never give up your faith. Believe God for better things.

"Whenever you stand praying, forgive, if you have anything against anyone, so that your Father who is in heaven will also forgive you your transgressions." Mark 11:25 NIV

If we forgive anyone who has offended us, God promises to answer our prayers.

Discover Your Purpose.

I came across a great email story (anonymous) that I thought really summed up what I have been saying throughout my book about what's "important" in life and thought you might like it. Hopefully it will help you discover your purpose in life. This is a story about what a 6-year old thinks is "A Dog's Purpose in Life."

A Dog's Purpose in Life?

(from the viewpoint of a 6-year-old as told by his dog's veterinarian)

Being a veterinarian, I had been called to examine a ten-year-old yellow Lab named Honey. The dog's owners, Ron, his wife Lisa and their little boy Shane, were all very attached to Honey, and they were hoping for a miracle.

I examined Honey and found he was dying of cancer. I told the family we couldn't do anything for Honey and offered to perform the euthanasia procedure in their home for the old dog.

As we made arrangements, Ron and Lisa told me they thought it would be good for six-year-old Shane to observe the procedure. They felt as though Shane might learn something from the experience.

The next day, I felt the familiar catch in my throat as Honey's family surrounded him. Shane seemed so calm, petting the old dog for the last time, that I wondered if he understood what was going on. Within a few minutes, Honey slipped peacefully away.

The little boy seemed to accept Honey's transition without any difficulty or confusion. We sat together for a while after Honey's death, wondering aloud about the sad fact that animal lives are shorter than human lives.

Shane, who had been listening quietly, piped up, "I know why."

Startled, we all turned to him. What came out of his mouth next stunned me. I'd never heard a more comforting explanation. It has changed the way I try and live.

He said, "People are born so that they can learn how to live a good life - like loving everybody all the time and being nice, right?" The six-year-old continued, "Well, dogs already know how to do that, so they don't have to stay as long."

What a simple statement that speaks volumes. You often hear the old saying "Out of the mouths of babes..." which actually comes from Matthew 21:16: ***"Jesus replied, "Haven't you ever read the Scriptures? For they say, 'You have taught children and infants to give you praise.'"***

The implication when we use that saying is that sometimes children have greater understanding than we would expect them to have or wisdom usually attributed to an adult. Examining the wisdom in Shane's statement, here is what I have noticed that dogs seem to "already know how to do:"

Live simply.

Love generously.

Care deeply.

Speak kindly.

Remember, if a dog was the teacher, you would learn things like:

When loved ones come home, always run to greet them.

Never pass up the opportunity to go for a joyride.

Allow the experience of fresh air and the wind in your face to be pure ecstasy.

Take naps.

Stretch before rising.

Run, romp and play daily.

Avoid biting when a simple growl will do.

On warm days, stop to lie on your back on the grass.

On hot days, drink lots of water and lie under a shady tree.

When you're happy, dance around and wag your entire body.

Delight in the simple joy of a long walk.

Be loyal.

Never pretend to be something you're not.

If what you want lies buried, dig until you find it.

When someone is having a bad day, be silent, sit close by and nuzzle them gently.

And most importantly, ALWAYS listen for the "Master's" voice and heed his commands enthusiastically.

There comes a time in life, when you walk away from all the drama and people who create it. You surround yourself with people who make you laugh, forget the bad and focus on the good. Remember, love the people who treat you right as well as those who don't. Think good thoughts for the ones who don't. Life is too short to be anything but happy. Falling down is part of LIFE...Getting back up is LIVING... so, if you want to find "purpose in life," live abundantly by applying these principles apparently "dogs already know how to do" and always listen for the Master's Voice and follow His Commands enthusiastically.

Loser or Winner? You Decide!

Without God, you become the master of your own destiny. Most people I have seen in life that do not have faith in a higher power than themselves, may appear successful and happy with their lives. But deep inside they lack real values that will determine if they are living for themselves or for others. Only God can guide and direct your paths and set you on a road of success that has real meaning, a road that leads you to help others and treat them with the dignity and respect they deserve. The suggested "**Action Plans**" I have set forth as guidelines for daily living involve principles and character traits that my peers, parents, teachers, coaches and others have instilled in me that enabled me to understand what is really important in life. Whether I have faced trials and tribulations, successes or failures, joy or sadness, winning or losing, I was taught during those times to always come out "a winner." What have I won? The game of life! No one will ever convince me that I am "a loser!" As you recall from an earlier quote, "God didn't create no junk!" I am not junk. You are not junk. None of us are destined to be losers. We are all winners when we let God determine who we are to become. My hope is that you will learn from my experiences and apply the principles you learn from this book. They will guide and direct you to a more fulfilling life, and you will not let negative outside influences lead you down the path of destruction, the path of a loser. I leave you with a promise and a commitment from Jesus' own words of doing your best for others and helping others in need!

The Promise:

"The thief comes only to steal and kill and destroy; I have come that they may have life, and have it to the full."

John 10:10 NIV

The Commitment for Life:

"Greater love has no one than this: to lay down one's life for one's friends."

John 15:13 NIV